Turning Knowledge into Income: Unlocking Earnings from Your Insights and Skills

Robert J. White

INTRODUCTION

Welcome to the transformative journey outlined in "Turning Knowledge into Income – Unlocking Earnings from Your Insights and Skills." This book is a compass guiding you through the intricate yet rewarding terrain of converting your expertise into a sustainable and thriving source of income.

In today's dynamic world, the value of your knowledge goes beyond mere information—it represents a potential revenue stream waiting to be tapped. The insights, skills, and experiences you possess are more than just assets; they are the building blocks for a lucrative financial future.

This comprehensive guide is designed to demystify the process of monetizing your expertise. It's more than a collection of strategies; it's a blueprint crafted to help you unravel the full potential of your skills and insights. From entrepreneurs seeking to leverage their unique offerings to professionals looking to amplify their income, this book is a gateway to exploring various avenues where your expertise can blossom into sustainable earnings.

You'll journey through the art of transforming what you know into a tangible source of revenue. Each chapter is a step forward, offering strategic insights, practical methodologies, and visionary approaches to empower you in crafting a solid income foundation. From understanding your unique expertise to identifying the right market demands and exploring diverse monetization avenues, this guide will lead you through a holistic journey of financial empowerment.

As you delve into the chapters, you'll embrace a philosophy that champions resilience, adaptability, and the spirit of innovation. You'll unearth the potential hidden within your expertise, cultivating a mindset that not only embraces change but thrives on innovation, and fosters the creation of your unique success story.

Get ready to embark on a transformative expedition. "Turning Knowledge Into Income" is your gateway to discovering the endless possibilities within your insights and skills, ultimately unlocking the doors to a future brimming with financial success and personal empowerment.

Chapter 1

Understanding Your Expertise

Leveraging your knowledge for financial gain begins with understanding your area of expertise. This chapter explores the significance of appreciating and appreciating the special worth of your abilities and insights. It invites introspection and facilitates the process of identifying your knowledge assets, which might include specialized information gained through school and experience as well as particular professional abilities.

This chapter helps you determine the scope and depth of your skill by focusing on self-awareness and introspection. It promotes a comprehensive assessment of your abilities, looking at how your knowledge and abilities might close gaps in particular markets or meet market demands. This chapter covers self-assessment techniques that will assist you in determining the breadth, depth, and practicality of your knowledge in a variety of settings.

The foundation for the next chapters is laid out in Understanding Your Expertise, which also frames the process of turning knowledge into a monetary income. It creates the crucial link between realizing the value of your abilities and insights and taking advantage of them, providing a strong starting point for the process of obtaining financial gain from your area of expertise.

Recognizing your knowledge Assets

The first step in making money out of your expertise is recognizing and identifying your knowledge assets. Your knowledge assets are made up of a wide range of perceptions, abilities, and experiences that are valuable in different situations. To properly exploit these assets for financial gain, it is necessary to comprehend and classify them.

Knowledge assets are fundamentally the result of your distinct experiences, education, abilities, and comprehension that you have accumulated throughout time. These are the intangible resources that have the potential to generate a sizable cash stream if they are identified and used effectively.

Self-reflection is one of the first steps in identifying your knowledge assets. Individuals are encouraged to evaluate their knowledge, abilities, and proficiency in a variety of fields through this introspective approach. It entails determining both transferable skills that might be useful in a variety of situations and specialized skills unique to a given sector or industry.

Think about your educational background, work history, and any particular training you may have received. Consider the distinct viewpoints you've acquired via the difficulties you've encountered or the sectors you've worked in. Your knowledge assets include your inventive thinking, problem-solving skills, and excellent communication abilities.

Furthermore, your interests and past experiences may contain special knowledge and abilities. For example, taking photos as a hobby may have sharpened your composition, detail, or storytelling skills. In a similar vein, your aptitude for experimentation, accuracy, and improvisation may have grown out of your love of cooking.

Finding your unique selling points and the qualities that add value to your insights is the first step in recognizing your knowledge assets. It's not just about degrees or certificates; it's about the special combination of your experiences and abilities that make up your area of competence.

Classifying and ranking your knowledge assets is the next step after outlining them. Take into account each asset's market value, significance, and demand. Determine which of your abilities or knowledge are most in demand or have the potential to address gaps in the market.

You can use this category to find possible industries or niches where your knowledge could be most useful. It makes it possible to take a more focused approach to monetization, concentrating on areas that most closely match your area of expertise and have the potential to yield larger rewards.

To sum up, identifying your knowledge assets involves more than just knowing what you know; it also involves realizing the potential worth that knowledge may have in a variety of situations. In order to monetize your expertise, you must first match your talents and insights with market demands. This process paves the way for a more focused and strategic approach to converting insights into revenue.

Assessing your skills and insights

A fundamental stage in the excursion of transforming information into pay is the exhaustive appraisal of your abilities and experiences. It includes a nitty gritty contemplation into the profundity, significance, and pertinence of the skill you have. This appraisal cycle expects to distinguish the particular qualities, shortcomings, and likely open doors inside your range of abilities and experiences, empowering you to use them for monetary benefit actually

- **Grasping the Profundity of Your Skills**
Begin by posting and classifying the abilities you have. These abilities might go from specialized capacities in a specific field to delicate abilities like correspondence, administration, or critical thinking. Survey the capability level and profundity of every expertise. Think about both your specialized capabilities and the less substantial yet similarly important delicate abilities, as they frequently

assume a critical part in different expert undertakings

- **Assessing the Pertinence and Applicability**

As you evaluate your abilities, think about their pertinence and appropriateness in various settings. A few abilities may be profoundly specific, principally reasonable for specific enterprises or specialties, while others could be more adaptable and versatile across different fields. Understanding where and how these abilities fit inside the market scene is vital. Evaluate the interest for these abilities, distinguish holes on the lookout, and perceive regions where your aptitude could be especially significant.

- **Divulging Your Interesting Insights**

Notwithstanding abilities, experiences and information acquired for a fact, training, or individual interest contribute essentially to your mastery. These experiences could incorporate exceptional points of view, imaginative methodologies, or explicit grasping gathered through your excursion. Perceive the particular perspectives or eccentric insight you offer of real value, as these can frequently be the differentiators that put you aside from others in your field.

- **Distinguishing Qualities and Tending to Weaknesses**

Direct a legitimate evaluation of your assets and shortcomings. Recognizing regions where you succeed permits you to use these qualities for adaptation. All the while, recognizing shortcomings is a chance for development or can direct your concentration towards ability improvement. It could likewise show expected coordinated efforts or regions where you really want extra help to augment your acquiring potential.

- **Adjusting Abilities and Experiences to Market Needs**

This evaluation interaction isn't exclusively about perceiving what you're great at; it's tied in with adjusting your abilities and experiences to advertise needs. Understanding how your mastery fills a hole or addresses an interest in the market is critical for effective adaptation. This arrangement is the way of offering arrangements or experiences that individuals will pay for.

All in all, surveying your abilities and experiences is a necessary piece of the excursion toward transforming information into pay. A pivotal step establishes the groundwork for the essential usage of your skill. Figuring out the profundity, pertinence, and uniqueness of your abilities and experiences is crucial in recognizing open doors and specialties where your insight can be adapted successfully. This interaction makes way for the resulting systems pointed toward augmenting income by sharing what you know.

Chapter 2

Identifying opportunities

Recognizing Open doors is a significant stage in the excursion of changing information into pay. This part is committed to uncovering the different roads and specialties where your ability can be important and adapted. It accentuates the investigation of chances that line up with your abilities, experiences, and the market interest.

Through a methodical methodology, this part directs you in perceiving the different open doors accessible for utilizing your skill. It supports a thorough examination of possible business sectors, enterprises, or explicit specialties that are needing your specific information or abilities. By understanding where your ability fits inside the market scene, you'll be prepared to recognize the most encouraging open doors for adaptation.

In addition, this part highlights the meaning of remaining versatile and open to arising potential open doors in different structures, for example, counseling, content creation, educating, or item improvement. It accentuates the significance of adjusting your skill to showcase requests, guaranteeing that the amazing open doors recognized can possibly create practical pay from your insight.

Recognizing Market Demand for Your Expertise

Understanding the market interest for your aptitude is a fundamental part in the excursion of changing over information into pay. Perceiving this request includes an extensive examination of the requirements, patterns, and holes inside unambiguous enterprises or specialties where your abilities and experiences can offer worth.

- **Exploring Industry Needs**
Start by leading intensive examination into the ventures or fields connected with your mastery.

Survey the latest things, challenges, and arising needs inside these areas. This examination helps in perceiving where your aptitude could give arrangements or satisfy existing requests.

- **Organizing and Conversations**

Take part in systems administration exercises and discussions inside proficient circles, online networks, or industry-explicit occasions. These connections give significant bits of knowledge into the ongoing prerequisites and expected open doors inside the business. Understanding the trouble spots or difficulties looked by experts or organizations can feature regions where your ability could be valuable.

- **Looking for Input and Validation**

Look for input from companions, coaches, or potential clients in regards to the importance and expected worth of your mastery. This approval interaction can affirm whether your abilities and experiences line up with the ongoing business sector interest. Criticism can likewise give fundamental direction to refining or fitting your contributions to more readily address the market's issues.

● Noticing Customer Behavior

Noticing customer conduct and market examples can offer significant bits of knowledge into what individuals are looking for and ready to pay for. Understanding buyer inclinations and ways of behaving inside the specialty connected with your skill is significant in distinguishing open doors for adaptation.

● Breaking down Contenders and Industry Landscape

Concentrate on contenders and existing players in your picked field. This investigation can uncover holes or regions where your skill could offer an exceptional viewpoint or arrangements not presently accessible. Separating your contributions from existing arrangements can give you an upper hand.

- **Utilizing Information and Analytics**

Use information and examination instruments to comprehend the quantitative parts of market interest. Investigating measurements, search patterns, or online entertainment commitment connected with your aptitude can offer experiences into the degree of premium and request inside your specialty.

- **Versatility and Flexibility**

Market requests aren't static. It develops with time and evolving needs. Being versatile and adaptable is fundamental in answering unique market requests. Embrace valuable open doors for persistent learning and improvement to remain significant in a moving scene.

All in all, perceiving market interest for your skill is significant for effective adaptation. This understanding permits you to situate your abilities and experiences in regions where they can offer the most benefit and produce manageable pay. By adjusting your skill to the particular necessities and requests of the market, you can actually use your insight to meet the prerequisites of your interest group, in this manner improving your true capacity for fruitful adaptation.

Exploring Income Avenues

As you adventure into adapting your skill, investigating different pay roads turns into a significant part of the excursion. Broadening revenue sources and recognizing numerous channels through which to use your insight expands your possibilities producing maintainable income. This part digs into the assorted roads accessible for making an interpretation of your mastery into unmistakable monetary returns.

* **Counseling and Warning Services**
Offering counseling or warning administrations in view of your mastery is a noticeable road. Giving direction, proposals, or key counsel to organizations or people looking for your

particular information can be a worthwhile pay source.

- **Instructing and Education**

Making courses, directing studios, or showing in your subject matter can be a compensating pay road. Whether through in-person meetings, online courses, or online courses, imparting your insight to enthusiastic students can bring about a predictable revenue source.

- **Content Creation**

Content creation through composition, contributing to a blog, vlogging, podcasting, or making other computerized content gives a road to share your bits of knowledge and contact a more extensive crowd. Utilizing stages like YouTube, Medium, or digital broadcast facilitating locales can transform your aptitude into monetizable substance.

- **Outsourcing and Agreement Work**

Offering your abilities and bits of knowledge on an independent or legally binding premise to people or organizations looking for explicit administrations can prompt a consistent pay. This could go from project-based work to offering specific types of assistance inside your mastery.

- **Item Improvement and Sales**

Creating and selling items in view of your skill, for example, digital books, programming, devices, or actual products, can make a wellspring of automated revenue. This road takes into account versatility and might possibly produce continuous income.

- **Speaking Commitment and Workshops**

Taking part in broad daylight talking about valuable open doors, leading studios, or taking an interest in industry occasions as a speaker can offer pay sources. These commitments give monetary advantages as well as lay out validity and grow your organization.

- **Authorizing and Partnerships**

Permitting your skill, whether it's as protected innovation, brand names, or licenses, permits others to involve your experiences for an expense. Furthermore, shaping associations or coordinated efforts inside your industry can bring about joint endeavors that create pay.

- **Online Stages and Marketplaces**

Utilizing on the web stages and commercial centers that take care of your skill can be a helpful method for interfacing with likely clients or clients. Stages like Upwork, Fiverr, or particular commercial centers for explicit businesses give open doors to adaptation.

- **Member Showcasing and Sponsorships**

Partaking in associate showcasing programs or getting sponsorships connected with your mastery can bring about extra pay. Elevating items or administrations to your crowd and procuring a commission or sponsorship expenses can be a significant revenue source.

All in all, investigating different pay roads extends the degree for changing over your mastery into pay. By enhancing your methodologies and being available across numerous revenue sources, you improve the probability of producing supportable income. Every road offers its interesting advantages and difficulties, permitting you to fit your adaptation approach as indicated by your mastery and crowd, eventually amplifying your true capacity for monetary returns.

Chapter 3

Building Your Monetization Strategy

"Building Your Monetization Strategy" is a significant section zeroed in on creating an extensive arrangement to change over your mastery into a maintainable pay successfully. This segment accentuates the efficient and vital methodology expected to adjust your abilities, bits of knowledge, and market interest with explicit adaptation techniques.

The part starts by directing you through an appraisal of your skill, market understanding, and favored pay roads. It helps with characterizing clear targets and putting forth attainable objectives in light of your mastery and the amazing open doors recognized. It then, at that point, digs into the most common way of choosing and focusing on the most appropriate adaptation techniques lined up with your skill and crowd.

Besides, this part stresses the meaning of an adaptable and versatile technique, taking into consideration trial and error and cycle as you test different adaptation strategies. It investigates the significance of refining your methodology in view of criticism, market changes, and advancing requests, guaranteeing that your adaptation technique stays dynamic and responsive.

Toward the finish of this section, you'll have an obvious and custom-made adaptation methodology, adjusting your abilities and experiences to explicit pay roads. This well thought out course of action will act as a guide, directing your activities as you progress toward expanding income from your mastery.

Creating a Monetization Roadmap

Creating a Monetization Roadmap is a fundamental part of successfully changing over your skill into a manageable pay. This cycle includes framing an organized arrangement that adjusts your abilities, bits of knowledge, and pay roads to accomplish your monetary objectives.

- **Characterize Your Targets and Goals**

Start by setting clear targets and characterizing feasible objectives. Distinguish what you plan to achieve with your adaptation endeavors. Whether it's procuring a particular pay target, laying down a good foundation for yourself as an industry authority, or making recurring sources of income, clearness on your goals is essential for creating an engaged guide.

- **Survey and Focus on Pay Avenues**

Evaluate the pay roads accessible in light of your skill and market interest. Focus on these roads in view of their achievability, possible returns, and arrangement with your goals. Consider which roads are generally reasonable for your mastery and where you can offer the most worth to your crowd.

- **Foster a Course of events and Milestones**

Make a timetable with feasible achievements that frame the means you'll take to adapt your mastery. Separate your goals into more modest, sensible undertakings. For example, on the off chance that content creation is one road, set achievements for the quantity of articles, recordings, or digital broadcasts you expect to deliver inside a particular time period.

- **Execute Broadening Strategies**

Broaden your revenue streams to alleviate hazards and improve possible profit. This could include joining different strategies, for example, counseling, content creation, instructing, and item improvement. Broadening offers strength and different income sources, decreasing reliance on a solitary revenue source.

- **Think about Present moment and Long haul Strategies**

Foster methodologies for both momentary additions and long haul maintainability. Momentary methodologies might incorporate fast wins or prompt pay producing activities, while long haul techniques center around building recurring, automated revenue sources or laying out serious areas of strength for a fore prosper.

- **Examine and Adjust In light of Feedback**

Incorporate a criticism circle into your guide. Break down the exhibition of every pay road and adjust your methodologies in view of criticism received from your crowd, market patterns, or the progress of your adaptation endeavors. This iterative methodology guarantees persistent improvement and advancement of your guide.

- **Embrace Adaptability and Experimentation**

Stay open to trial and error and adaptability inside your guide. As the market develops, new open doors arise, and crowd inclinations change.

Embrace this by testing new techniques, changing your systems, and investigating creative ways to deal with advancing your adaptation endeavors.

- **Track Progress and Change Accordingly**

Routinely keep tabs on your development against the set achievements and targets. Screen the progress of every pay road and change your systems in a like manner. This following system guarantees that you remain on track and pursue informed choices to amplify your income.

All in all, making an adaptation guide fills in as an organized arrangement directing your endeavors to change over your mastery into pay successfully. By setting clear targets, focusing on pay roads, laying out a course of events, and consolidating versatility, your guide turns into a powerful device, guaranteeing constant advancement towards your monetary objectives. This essential methodology permits you to zero in on activities that line up with your mastery and crowd, eventually boosting the potential for fruitful adaptation.

Choosing the Right Platforms and Methods

Choosing the fitting stages and strategies for adapting your mastery is a significant part of your excursion towards creating supportable pay. This cycle includes key decision-production to recognize the most fitting channels and procedures that line up with your abilities, bits of knowledge, and crowd.

- **Figuring out Stage Suitability**

Start by evaluating different stages accessible for sharing your skill. Think about internet based stages, commercial centers, virtual entertainment, and particular industry channels. Pick stages in light of their importance to your ability, the arrival they offer, and their reasonableness for drawing in with your interest group.

- **Recognizing the Right Methods**

Investigate and evaluate the assorted adaptation strategies accessible. Consider techniques, for example, counseling, instructing, content creation, item advancement, or other explicit strategies lined up with your aptitude. Select strategies that resound with your abilities and can actually make an interpretation of your insight into pay.

- **Assess Crowd Preferences**

Grasp the inclinations of your crowd. Break down where they like to consume data or administrations connected with your mastery. Think about their favored organizations (recordings, articles, courses) and stages (YouTube, Medium, online courses, and so on.). This examination will direct you in picking techniques and stages that take special care of your crowd's inclinations.

- **Evaluating Business sector Trends**

Remain refreshed on market patterns and industry shifts. Pick stages and techniques that are in accordance with current market drifts and can possibly build up some forward movement later on. For example, on the off chance that there's an arising interest for particular kinds of content or administrations in your specialty, consider integrating these patterns into your methodology.

- **Utilizing Specialty explicit Platforms**

Investigate specialty explicit stages or networks pertinent to your aptitude. These stages frequently offer a designated crowd keen on specific information. By drawing in with these networks, you can lay out validity and access a more engaged crowd energetic for your experiences.

- **Balance Your Approach**

Make progress toward a decent methodology while choosing stages and strategies. Consider a mix of stages and strategies to enhance your revenue sources. For example, in the event that content creation is your essential technique, investigate different stages (online journals, web-based entertainment, digital broadcasts) to contact a more extensive crowd and increment pay potential.

- **Testing and Iteration**

Test various stages and strategies to distinguish the best ones for adapting your mastery. Carry out systems across different stages and techniques, then, at that point, break down the outcomes. In light of this examination, refine your methodology, disposing of less compelling techniques and enhancing those yielding improved results.

- **Long haul Reasonability and Scalability**

Think about the drawn out suitability and versatility of the picked stages and strategies. Assess whether these decisions can support your pay objectives over the long run and take into consideration development. Decide on techniques and stages that offer the potential for persistent development and extension.

All in all, picking the right stages and strategies assumes an imperative part in effective adaptation. By decisively adjusting your skill to reasonable stages and strategies, you can really contact your crowd, create pay, and lay out a supportable adaptation model. This choice cycle, when combined with flexibility and an eagerness to explore, guarantees you're expanding your true capacity for transforming your insight into a reliable revenue source.

Chapter 4

Leveraging Your Knowledge for Profit

"Leveraging Your Knowledge for Profit" centers around changing your skill into a worthwhile revenue source. This part rotates around essential strategies and approaches pointed toward amplifying the worth of your abilities, bits of knowledge, and encounters to produce critical monetary returns.

The part starts by investigating the different ways of situating and exhibiting your mastery. It digs into content creation, offering experiences on making high-esteem content to dazzle your crowd. In addition, it examines the significance of laying out validity and authority, empowering you to really use your insight.

Moreover, this section tends to techniques to adapt your mastery through educating, counseling, and item improvement. It guides you through the most common way of changing your abilities into administrations, courses, or items, at last empowering you to benefit from your novel information and experiences.

Toward the finish of this part, you'll have a thorough comprehension of how to decisively use your insight to produce benefit. It offers significant bits of knowledge and methodologies to situate yourself really inside your industry or specialty, guaranteeing that your skill turns into an important resource adding to your monetary achievement.

Content Creation: Sharing Your Expertise

Content creation fills in as a strong vehicle for sharing your mastery and transforming it into a significant kind of revenue. Whether through composition, recordings, webcasts, or different structures, making content empowers you to contact a wide crowd, lay out power, and adapt your insight really.

- **Distinguishing Content Platforms**

Pick the stages that adjust best to your skill and crowd. This could be a blog, YouTube channel, digital broadcast series, or virtual entertainment stages. Select stages where your crowd is probably going to draw in with and consume your substance.

- **Making Significant and Applicable Content**

Convey content that offers genuine worth to your crowd. This could be as enlightening articles, how-to guides, savvy recordings, or intriguing webcasts. Content ought to be pertinent to your ability, tending to the trouble spots or interests of your crowd.

- **Consistency and Quality**

Consistency is key in happy creation. Consistently distributing top caliber, educational, and drawing in satisfied forms a devoted crowd.

Make progress toward higher expectations when in doubt, guaranteeing that each piece of content adds esteem and keeps an exclusive requirement.

- **Laying out Power and Credibility**

Utilize content creation as a device to lay out experts in your field. Offer extraordinary bits of knowledge, share encounters, and give answers for normal issues inside your mastery. Steady conveyance of excellent substance constructs believability, situating you as a confided in a wellspring of data.

- **Connecting with Your Audience**

Energize crowd commitment by answering remarks, questions, and input. Effectively draw in with your crowd to encourage a local area and construct compatibility. This association can likewise give experiences into the inclinations and necessities of your crowd, directing your substance creation endeavors.

- **Adaptation Potential open doors inside Content**

Investigate different ways of adapting your substance. This could incorporate offshoot showcasing, sponsorships, promotions, or in any event, offering premium substance through memberships or participations. Utilizing your crowd's trust can prompt pay open doors as you suggest or give items or administrations connected with your ability.

- **Expansion and Experimentation**

Enhance your substance arrangements and attempt new methodologies. Try different things with various substance types to find what reverberates most with your crowd. You could investigate digital books, online courses, contextual analyses, or meetings to enhance and grow your substance contributions.

- **Upgrading for Search and Visibility**

Upgrade your substance for web crawlers to further develop perceivability. Utilize Web optimization best practices by utilizing pertinent catchphrases, upgrading meta labels, and making content that gives arrangements or replies to normal inquiries inside your mastery.

- **Estimating Achievement and Iterating**

Consistently track your substance's presentation utilizing investigation apparatuses. Examine measurements like perspectives, commitment, changes, and crowd socioeconomics. In view of this information, refine and emphasize your substance procedure to work on its effect and viability.

In rundown, content creation is an integral asset for sharing your skill and adapting your insight. By reliably delivering important, great substance and drawing in with your crowd, you can lay out power, fabricate a dependable following, and make different revenue streams from your mastery. This road permits you to share bits of knowledge as well as positions you as a go-to asset inside your field, contributing essentially to your monetary achievement.

Establishing Credibility and Authority

Establishing credibility and authority inside your field is critical in utilizing your aptitude for monetary profit. This cycle includes purposeful activities that form trust, show your mastery, and position you as a regarded figure in your industry or specialty.

- **Convey Steady Value**

Consistency in offering important and dependable data is vital. Guarantee that your substance, counsel, or administrations reliably offer certifiable benefit and assist with taking care of issues or address needs inside your subject matter.

- **Exhibit Skill and Experience**

Feature your aptitude through different mediums. Whether through happy creation, public talking, industry occasions, or commitments to distributions, grandstand your insight and experience to your crowd. Contextual analyses, examples of overcoming adversity, or tributes can act as important evidence of your abilities

- **Organizing and Collaboration**

Team up and draw in with different experts in your field. Joining forces with laid out figures, adding to cooperative undertakings, or taking part in board conversations can upgrade your perceivability and believability. Organizing inside your industry approves your standing and aptitude.

- **Instructive Substance and Thought Leadership**

Express impression administration content that goes past essential data. Give inside and out examination, exceptional viewpoints, and creative answers for industry challenges. Interesting substance positions you as a specialist and industry pioneer.

- **Tributes and Reviews**

Accumulate tributes or surveys from clients, partners, or the people who have profited from your ability. Certifiable and positive criticism upgrades believability, consoling expected clients or crowd individuals from the worth you give.

- **Consistent Learning and Improvement**

Show a pledge to progressing learning and improvement. Remain refreshed with industry patterns, new turns of events, and arising procedures inside your field. Sharing your commitment to persistent improvement upgrades your believability as a groundbreaking master.

- **Validness and Transparency**

Be legitimate and straightforward in your connections. Certified and legitimate correspondence with your crowd encourages trust. Conceding botches, sharing encounters, and being straightforward about your process adapts your picture and builds up believability.

- **Public Talking and Engagements**

Participate in broad daylight talking about valuable open doors, studios, or online classes inside your field. Sharing your insight in open discussions lays out your aptitude as well as widens your compass and impact.

- **Confirmations and Qualifications**

Getting important certificates or capabilities inside your field can add believability. Formal capabilities or accreditations from perceived foundations approve your aptitude and give extra confirmation to your crowd.

- **Commitment and Local area Building**

Effectively draw in with your crowd or local area. Answer requests, take part in conversations, and give direction. Building a local area around your mastery cultivates trust and positions you as a dependable wellspring of data.

Laying out believability and authority takes time and predictable exertion. By exhibiting your mastery, giving significant and credible substance, and drawing in with your crowd and industry peers, you can make major areas of strength for a. After some time, this standing as a believable and definitive figure in your field will prompt expanded trust and, at last, extended open doors for adapting your insight.

Chapter 5

Monetization Tools and Techniques

"Monetization Tools and Techniques" dives into the useful strategies and stages that empower the change of mastery into pay. This segment investigates a variety of instruments and techniques intended to adapt your insight and bits of knowledge successfully. It centers around the utilization of these devices to amplify acquiring potential in different revenue sources.

The section covers a scope of devices and strategies, for example, partner showcasing, online courses, participation locales, counseling stages, internet business arrangements, publicizing organizations, and other adaptation techniques. It frames the advantages, execution systems, and best practices for each instrument or method, intending to give a complete comprehension of how to use these assets to produce pay from your skills.

Monetization Platforms and Tools

Monetization Platforms and Tools offer different chances to change skill into a worthwhile revenue source. These devices and stages assume a huge part in working with the most common way of coming to, drawing in, and adapting your crowd or clients. Understanding and actually using these assets is fundamental for expanding the monetary capability of your insight and experiences.

- **Web based business Platforms**

Stages like Shopify, WooCommerce, or Etsy give a road to sell items or administrations in view of your mastery. Whether it's computerized products, products, or administrations, web based business stages empower you to set up internet based stores and contact a worldwide crowd.

- **Enrollment and Membership Services**

Instruments like Patreon, Substack, or Memberful permit you to make participation or membership based models, offering elite substance or administrations to endorsers. These stages empower you to fabricate a dedicated following and procure repeating pay by giving premium substance or administrations.

- **Counseling and Independent Platforms**

Stages like Upwork, Fiverr, or Catalant take care of offering counseling or independent administrations. These stages interface you with clients looking for explicit aptitude, permitting you to adapt your abilities through projects or counseling commitment.

- **Online Course and Learning Platforms**

Sites like Udemy, Workable, or Coursera empower you to make and sell online courses. These stages give an organized climate to sharing information, directing courses, and adapting your skill through instructive substance.

- **Subsidiary Promoting Networks**

Subsidiary organizations like Amazon Partners, ShareASale, or CJ Member permit you to advance items or administrations connected with your skill. By prescribing or supporting items to your crowd, you procure a commission for every deal made through your outside reference.

- **Promoting Organizations and Sponsorships**

Stages like Google AdSense, Mediavine, or sponsorship amazing open doors through web recordings or recordings empower you to procure pay through notices. These stages associate you with publicists or patrons looking to contact your crowd.

- **Content Adaptation Platforms**

Content-based stages like Medium's Accomplice Program, YouTube's Accomplice Program, or Substack's paid bulletins empower you to adapt explicit sorts of content. These projects pay makers in light of elements like perspectives, commitment, or memberships.

- **Protected innovation Authorising Platforms**

Sites like Shutterstock or iStockPhoto permit you to adapt your skill through authorizing protected innovation, like photos or designs. By transferring and authorizing your manifestations, you can procure sovereignties each time your work is utilized or bought.

- **Digital recording Adaptation Platforms**

Digital recording explicit stages like Anchor, Podbean, or Patreon offer instruments to adapt your webcasts. These stages work with audience support, sponsorship open doors, or membership based content to produce digital recording related pay.

- **Virtual Entertainment and Local area Monetization**

Virtual entertainment stages like Facebook Gatherings, Jerk, or Patreon People group empower local area based adaptation. By offering selective substance, commitment, or advantages to your local area individuals, you can acquire pay.

Understanding and decisively using these adaptation stages and devices turn out assorted revenue streams. By joining and utilizing these assets successfully, you can enhance your income and make a feasible income model from your skill. Every stage and device offers novel open doors, permitting you to fit your way to deal with best suit your ability and crowd.

Strategies for Maximizing Earnings

Strategies for Maximizing Earnings from your skill envelop a far reaching approach that coordinates different strategies, instruments, and shrewd practices to enhance your pay potential. Executing these techniques permits you to adapt your insight and experiences actually

- **Enhancement and Different Revenue Streams**

One of the best techniques is to broaden your revenue sources. Rather than depending on a solitary kind of revenue, investigate different roads, for example, counseling, content creation, courses, items, and administrations. Broadening spreads hazard and upgrades generally speaking profit potential.

- **Center around High-Worth Offerings**

Underline high-esteem contributions that line up with your mastery and take care of the particular necessities of your crowd. By zeroing in on high-esteem administrations, items, or content, you can order premium costs, bringing about higher pay

- **Constant Improvement and Education**

Put resources into constant learning and improvement inside your field. Remaining refreshed with the most recent patterns, new turns of events, and arising strategies permits you to offer state of the art administrations, keeping you ahead and legitimizing higher rates for your skill.

- **Key Valuing and Packaging**

Painstakingly set costs and bundle your contributions. Consider estimating your administrations or items in view of their worth as opposed to exclusively on industry norms. Explore different avenues regarding different estimating models to track down the ideal harmony among worth and moderateness.

- **Proficient Using time effectively and Scalability**

Execute successful time usage rehearses. Smooth out your cycles and distinguish assignments that can be robotized or rethought, empowering you to zero in on high-esteem exercises. Versatility guarantees you can grow your pay potential without proportionately expanding time or exertion.

- **Showcasing and Brand Building**

Put resources into promoting and brand building endeavors. Laying out serious areas of strength for an and really promoting your mastery permits you to contact a more extensive crowd. A strategically set up brand draws in additional clients and clients, adding to expanded profit.

- **Organizing and Partnerships**

Influence organizing potential open doors and look for associations inside your industry. Teaming up with different specialists, powerhouses, or organizations can grow your span and lead to new pay potential open doors.

- **Client Maintenance and Upselling**

Center around holding existing clients and upselling extra items or administrations. Offering amazing assistance and sustaining associations with your clients can bring about repeating pay from fulfilled clients.

- **Iterative Methodology and Information Analysis**

Take on an iterative way to deal with your procedures. Routinely dissect information from your revenue sources, crowd commitment, and market patterns. In view of this examination, change and work on your procedures for better monetary results.

- **Risk The board and Adaptability**

Be ready for dangers and market vacillations. Guarantee that you are versatile and adaptable in your methodology. Enhancement of revenue sources and consistent improvement methodologies go about as a type of chance administration.

Executing these methodologies by and large improves your capacity to augment income from your aptitude. By embracing a comprehensive methodology that consolidates enhancement, vital evaluating, constant improvement, and compelling showcasing, you can make a strong pay model that streamlines your procuring potential. These techniques engage you to successfully adapt your insight, guaranteeing a supportable and remunerating monetary profit from your master

Chapter 6

Overcoming Challenges

"Overcoming Challenges" addresses the obstacles and hindrances experienced while adapting skill. This part gives direction on exploring and overcoming normal difficulties in the excursion towards changing over information into pay. It examines procedures for conquering issues like market vacillations, finding the right crowd, rivalry, supporting revenue sources, adjusting time, and overseeing vulnerabilities. This section plans to furnish perusers with apparatuses, attitude, and systems to handle these difficulties actually, encouraging strength and flexibility chasing monetary accomplishment from their skill.

Addressing Common Hurdles

Addressing Common Hurdles is a fundamental part of the excursion to really adapt ability.

While seeking monetary accomplishment from your insight, different difficulties might emerge. By distinguishing and tending to these normal obstacles, you can proactively explore through possible deterrents and streamline your way to progress.

- **Market Changes and Trends**

One test includes market changes and patterns. Enterprises continually advance, and it is pivotal to figure out these movements. Address this by remaining informed, being versatile, and enhancing revenue streams to alleviate the effect of changing economic situations.

- **Tracking down the Right Audience**

Recognizing and contacting the right crowd can be a test. Research and investigate your objective segment completely. Tailor your informing, content, and contributions to take care of the requirements and inclinations of your optimal crowd.

- **Contest and Differentiation**

Hang out in a cutthroat scene by zeroing in on what makes your mastery exceptional. Feature your particular incentive and look for ways of separating your contributions. Address this obstacle by stressing your assets and conveying high-esteem, unrivaled administrations or content.

- **Consistency and Sustainability**

Consistency in happy creation or administration arrangement can be challenging. Execute methodologies like preparing, setting plans, and keeping a substance schedule. Consistency constructs trust and keeps your crowd drawn in, adding to supported revenue sources.

- **Using time effectively and Prioritization**

Adjusting different revenue sources or errands can overpower. Foster viable time usage procedures and focus on high-esteem errands. Delegate or robotize monotonous assignments to zero in on high-influence exercises that produce pay.

- **Monetary Vulnerability and Risks**

Monetary vulnerability and dangers are innate in business. Relieve these difficulties by keeping a monetary wellbeing net, differentiating pay sources, and persistently checking and changing techniques in light of market changes

- **Adjusting to Innovation and Tools**

Innovation continually develops, and adjusting to new instruments or stages can be a test. Focus profoundly on understanding and utilizing arising innovations or instruments applicable to your mastery. Constant learning and trial and error with new instruments can yield higher efficiency and pay.

- **Client Maintenance and Satisfaction**

Keeping up with it is fundamental to fulfill clients or clients. Offer outstanding assistance, be receptive to input, and spotlight on building enduring connections. Focusing on consumer loyalty upgrades faithfulness and builds the potential for rehash business or references.

- **Self-Uncertainty and Confidence**

Trust in your mastery can vary, prompting self-question. Address this test by zeroing in on persistent picking up, praising accomplishments, looking for help from coaches or networks, and understanding that skill develops over the long haul.

- **Lawful and Managerial Hurdles**

Exploring lawful or managerial systems may be perplexing. Look for proficient counsel, figure out the legalities in your industry, and guarantee consistent guidelines. Clear getting it and consistency forestall possible difficulties.

By tending to these normal obstacles chasing adapting ability, you invigorate your excursion towards monetary achievement. Utilizing proactive systems, flexibility, and a persistent learning outlook permits you to explore difficulties successfully and improve your way to transforming your insight into a supportable and compensating pay.

Managing Risks and Obstacles

Managing risks and obstacles is urgent during the time spent adapting mastery, guaranteeing a maintainable pay stream and fruitful profession improvement. Really taking care of these difficulties considers a safer and versatile way to deal with utilizing information for monetary profit.

- **Distinguishing Possible Risks**

Start by recognizing potential dangers that could influence your revenue sources. This could incorporate market variances, evolving patterns, mechanical interruptions, lawful or administrative changes, or contests inside your speciality

- **Risk Evaluation and Analysis**

Direct an exhaustive gamble appraisal and examination to assess the possible effect of distinguished chances. Decide the probability of events and the seriousness of their effect on your pay and in general business technique.

- **Foster Gamble Alleviation Strategies**

Whenever gambles are distinguished and investigated, foster techniques to moderate these difficulties. This could incorporate enhancing revenue sources, making a monetary wellbeing net, adjusting to showcase moves, or creating emergency courses of action.

- **Broadening of Revenue Streams**

Broaden revenue streams to lessen reliance on a solitary source. Having various income sources guarantees that assuming one stream is influenced, others can give security. This could include offering various administrations, items, or investigating shifted adaptation techniques.

- **Nonstop Learning and Adaptation**

Remain refreshed and consistently advance inside your field to expect and adjust to changing patterns and innovations. This proactive methodology helps in remaining in front of possible disturbances and adjusting to new open doors.

- **Monetary Preparation and Possibility Funds**

Lay out a sound monetary arrangement and make possibility reserves. These assets act as a support during lean periods or unforeseen crises, giving monetary security and strength in the midst of precariousness.

- **Legitimate and Consistency Measures**

Stick to legitimate and administrative necessities inside your industry. Understanding and consistency with legalities diminish the gamble of confronting lawful difficulties that could influence pay age.

- **Organizing and Partnerships**

Building areas of strength for an and framing vital organizations offers extra help. Teaming up with industry peers or shaping unions gives admittance to assets, backing, and valuable open doors, lessening individual gamble factors.

- **Protection and Expert Support**

Consider protection or expert help to alleviate explicit dangers. For example, responsibility protection, licensed innovation assurance, or looking for legitimate and monetary counsel can add an additional layer of security.

- **Checking and Adaptability**

Consistently screen your techniques and execution, adjusting as needs be. Survey and rethink your gamble on the board systems routinely to guarantee they line up with your objectives and the developing business climate.

Overseeing dangers and snags is a continuous interaction that requires ingenuity, versatility, and a groundbreaking mentality. By recognizing expected gambles, executing relief procedures, and consistently adjusting to transforms, you reinforce your capacity to support and develop your pay from mastery, making a safer and versatile starting point for long haul monetary achievement.

Chapter 7

Scaling and Growing Your Income Stream

Scaling and Growing Your Income Stream centers around procedures and systems to grow and upgrade the adaptation of your mastery. This part investigates strategies to increment pay sources, expand crowd reach, and upgrade existing income streams. It digs into scaling through differentiated contributions, venturing into new business sectors, utilizing innovation, and integrating productive frameworks and cycles. The section plans to direct users on taking their revenue streams to a higher level by deliberately extending their chances, cultivating development, and guaranteeing supportability in their monetary development venture.

Scaling Strategies for Long-term Success

Scaling strategies are fundamental for long-term success in adapting ability, guaranteeing supported development and expanded revenue streams over the long haul. Executing these systems considers extension, broadening, and enhancement, making a vigorous starting point for proceeding with monetary achievement.

- **Expansion and Different Revenue Streams**

Persistently expand pay sources to diminish reliance on a solitary income stream. Investigate different roads, for example, counseling, content creation, courses, items, and administrations. Expansion spreads hazard and improves in general profit potential.

- **Robotize and Systemize**

Foster productive frameworks and cycles to robotize routine assignments, considering additional opportunity to zero in on high-esteem exercises. Computerization and systemization smooth out tasks and scale your business without a corresponding expansion in exertion.

- **Versatile Business Models**

Make versatile plans of action that can develop without dramatically inflating costs. Consider models that extend effectively, for example, membership based administrations, online courses, or versatile items that can be sold without huge manual in information

- **Venture into New Business sectors or Niches**

Investigate venture into new business sectors or specialties connected with your ability. Extending your compass permits you to take advantage of undiscovered crowds or ventures, possibly opening up new revenue sources and expansion open doors.

- **Influence Innovation and Innovation**

Remain refreshed with mechanical headways and embrace imaginative apparatuses or stages that line up with your ability. Utilizing innovation can fundamentally upgrade efficiency and reach, supporting scaling activities and pay potential.

- **Vital Associations and Collaborations**

Look for associations or joint efforts inside or outside your industry. Teaming up with different specialists or organizations offers admittance to new business sectors, assets, and skill, cultivating versatility and development.

- **Center around High-Worth Offerings**

Underline high-esteem contributions and premium administrations that line up with your mastery. This approach positions you in a space where you can order higher rates, at last prompting expanded pay.

- **Persistent Learning and Adaptation**

Keep a development mentality and focus on nonstop learning. Staying versatile to showcase changes, patterns, and new open doors permits you to proactively scale your aptitude and pay potential.

- **Client Driven Approach**

Focus on consumer loyalty and maintenance. Fulfilled clients lead to rehash business, references, and potential for upselling extra administrations, adding to supported pay development.

- **Information Driven Choice Making**

Use information examination to drive choices. Screen execution measurements, crowd conduct, and market patterns to distinguish potential open doors for development and refinement in your pay procedures.

Executing these scaling procedures takes into account consistent and maintainable development, growing your revenue sources and cementing long haul achievement. By enhancing, systemizing, improving, and adjusting to developing business sector requests, you sustain your situation in adapting mastery and guarantee a safer and productive future.

Expanding and Diversifying Your Income

Expanding and diversifying income sources is an essential methodology that improves monetary soundness and long haul achievement while adapting skill. It includes widening income streams through different techniques, offering a cushion against market changes and setting out various open doors for money age.

- **Investigate New Avenues**

Look past existing pay sources to find new roads for adapting your aptitude. This could include fanning out into various administrations, items, or businesses connected with your field of information.

- **Make Various Income Streams**

Lay out numerous revenue streams by offering a scope of items or administrations. Consider broadening into counseling, training, computerized items, actual product, studios, or online courses, taking care of various crowd needs and inclinations.

- **Use Stage Diversity**

Investigate different stages to expand pay potential. Utilize web-based entertainment, online business destinations, independent stages, participation based networks, and content-sharing stages to expand your presence and contact various crowds.

- **Recurring, automated revenue Opportunities**

Present recurring, automated revenue open doors, for example, digital books, computerized items, or associate advertising. When made, these sources keep on producing pay without the requirement for consistent dynamic inclusion.

- **Venture into New Business sectors or Demographics**

Consider contacting new business sectors or socioeconomics. Tailor your contributions to address the issues of various client sections or enterprises inside your skill, extending your client base and pay potential

- **Influence Existing Expertise**

Use your current skill to offer new or particular administrations. For example, on the off chance that you are an essayist, consider fanning into copywriting, altering, or educational plan in view of your composing abilities.

- **Center around High-Worth Administrations or Products**

Underline high-esteem administrations or items that adjust intimately with your skill. These exceptional contributions frequently permit you to order higher rates and create more critical pay.

- **Make Repeating Income Models**

Execute membership based administrations or participations. These models make unsurprising and predictable pay by offering progressing benefits to supporters.

- **Team up and Partner**

Accomplice or team up with different specialists or organizations. These partnerships frequently set out new open doors, offer admittance to more extensive organizations, and grow your pay potential.

- **Adjust to Arising Trends**

Keep up to date with arising patterns in your field. Expect and adjust your contributions to these patterns, permitting you to be at the cutting edge of industry changes and gain by new open doors.

Extending and broadening pay sources gives versatility against market moves and fortifies your monetary position. By embracing numerous income streams, investigating new business sectors, and offering a scope of high-esteem administrations or items, you make a more steady and productive pay structure from your mastery. This approach grows procuring potential as well as guarantees a safer and reasonable monetary future

Conclusion

In the amazing orchestra of turning knowledge into income, each note played implies commitment, imagination, and a steadfast soul. As the last shade slips on this improving excursion, recall this: the combination of mastery and profit isn't simply a monetary triumph; it's an odyssey set apart by inventiveness, versatility, and an unfaltering obligation to development.

This journey is a lively material where learning blends with development, where flexibility hits the dance floor with an open door, and where the seeds of progress are planted in the rich ground of enthusiasm and diligence. It's a demonstration of the craft of transforming what you know into a work of art that resounds with genuineness and worth.

As you track the way ahead, let your insight be the directing star, lighting the way to new skylines. Embrace change as a buddy, development as a torchbearer, and advancement as a foundation of your excursion. Etch in your heart the song of consumer loyalty and the cadence of industry patterns, for they will fit into an orchestra that resonates with progress.

Keep in mind, your skill isn't just an item yet a reference point enlightening ways, tackling issues, and upgrading lives. This endeavor is a continuous crescendo, an elating crescendo toward a future where each illustration took in, each challenge survived, and each achievement celebrated turns into a melodic stanza in the ensemble of your victorious skill. Thus, walk ahead with conviction, hit the dance floor with open doors, and coordinate a finale that resounds with the reverberations of your improved skill, for the world enthusiastically anticipates your one of a kind song of progress.